ON TEACHING GENEALOGY

ON TEACHING GENEALOGY

By Fran Carter

American Genealogical Lending Library

Bountiful, Utah

American Genealogical Lending Library, P.O. Box 244, Bountiful, Utah 84011

Printed in the United States of America
97 96 95 94 93 7 6 5 4 3 2

ISBN 0-945433-05-0

CONTENTS

FOREWORD

Genealogy, in the last decade, has become America's favorite *indoor* sport. Devotees know well that the pursuit of their favorite sport demands much running - to libraries, archives, courthouses, cemeteries. Increasingly they become aware that no one source, human or archival, has all the answers they seek, so they join genealogical societies to share information, take courses, and attend conferences and seminars.

Whether you are beginning to look for your ancestors or have acquired expertise from years of research, you are aware that there is more to learn. You join a society and discover that it is made up of individuals like yourself, amateurs at various stages of research. In your eagerness you may become an active member of your society and learn, as so many have, that the society is only as good as the knowledge it can supply to individual members.

Fran Carter has written a book that can make your society meaningful, because it helps YOU not only learn, but teach genealogy. There are many individuals in the field who call themselves *teachers*, most of them self-taught. Here in one volume, you can find the techniques, the sources, the methods to becoming an effective teacher.

Written in the forthright style that is characteristic of this effervescent former high school teacher and mother of six, it is full of fascinating suggestions that can make your genealogical society into a teaching organization, and strengthen it by involving every member's talents. Your teachers and the seminars you attend are required to be on their toes to answer the questions Fran recommends that you ask.

And your diploma? Not a paper or parchment certificate, but a better route to roots for you and for those who benefit from *ON TEACHING GENEALOGY.*

New York
April 1989

Rabbi Malcolm H. Stern
Past president and Fellow
American Society of Genealogists
Board member, Federation of Genealogical Societies

PREFACE

There has been little in the field of genealogy concerning the teaching of the subject. This material is designed to give you some clues that you may need to teach that subject. The actual teaching you will need to do yourself.

Everyone who is involved in the practice of genealogy is teaching someone else about the subject, simply by the way they respond to questions and share their knowledge.

The teacher of genealogy is probably not a professional in the field, nor is he usually trained in the field of teaching. But he DOES have genealogical history experience and expertise in the field. Teaching this subject may be a part- time avocation, grown out of a hobby in some situations.

Those who find themselves in the classroom soon find that genealogy teachers are MADE not BORN. Usually a person is working on his own genealogy, has a few lucky breaks, gets interested enough to accumulate some excellent books and materials, tries a couple of new ideas, and suddenly that person is an "expert!" SOMEONE decides that this person "knows" so much more than they do (which they usually don't), and asks that person to teach a class. It is up to that teacher to search out the tools and resources that prove that genealogy teachers are MADE. The basic knowledge is there, the teaching skills may need help.

The suggestions in this book consist of a few pages of pointers on sharing your knowledge; written in simple, practical, easy-to-read style in non-academic language, to give you the confidence needed for teaching.

The REASON for a book on TEACHING GENEALOGY, is the need to promote growth of the organization (hereafter called a society). It is indeed rare to find a group that would define its problem as too rapid growth, although that does exist. Declining or stagnant membership is usually listed as a major problem in the society of under 300 membership. Identifying that problem and facing that fact, there can be but one answer -- EDUCATION, EDUCATION, EDUCATION. That is what this book is all about. This section addresses the rationale that is needed to make the decision that your organization needs an educational program.

The plans and ideas here are put forth that you might study the reasons behind the question -- WHY EDUCATION?

Any level genealogist needs education. The more experienced the genealogist, the more convinced he is that the answer lies in education. The more that is known about the subject, the quicker personal questions can be answered. The experienced genealogist is always searching for that buried tidbit that will unravel his own personal problem.

The beginner still may be at the stage of not knowing what questions to ask, whereas the more advanced student asks more specific questions. However, our aim here is to define the growth problems within a society and your answer is EDUCATION.

Every new beginner or advanced student that is taught by your local society becomes a new active member who needs to continue his educational growth. If a society does not supply that education, these members are soon lost. The responsibility lies with the society to sponsor or co-sponsor or initiate educational programs. Your group may work through local educational groups as co-sponsor, but those classes need your support.

There are all kinds of groups offering help when programs are in the planning stages. This advice is given free of charge by your state organization, FEDERATION OF GENEALOGICAL SOCIETIES (see addresses elsewhere) and others. The journals, professional publications and newsletters offer ideas of what others are doing.

Education, in the genealogical field, comes in many forms; from a simple -- BRING A FRIEND TO MEETING, SPECIAL GUESTS, to the other end of the spectrum of intensive seminars -- and everything in between.

If your society has reviewed its needs carefully and agreed that education should be a major part of its long range planning/goals, you may want to form a special planning committee, one that would have a good understanding of the history of your group and knowledge of your official structure. This group would study and proceed with a plan or goal for the future. There would probably be at least two major ideas brought forth in its thinking:

1. A NUMERICAL GROWTH OF MEMBERS

2. EDUCATIONAL GROWTH OF MEMBERS

These two topics go hand-in-hand. Education means growth.

In choosing the line of education as your goal, and numerical growth as a long range plan, you need to seriously think of offering a BASIC/BEGINNER class AT LEAST ONCE A YEAR. To keep bringing in new people, classes are a necessity, and they should be taught year after year.

So as not to neglect the member who has been working for years and years, choose classes to meet his needs. There may be a need without a local teacher available. If this is the case, review this material carefully. It may give you ideas on how to fill that need.

TRY to use your own members for teaching. Have you ASKED? Each one, by contributing to an organization, has the feeling that he really belongs to that group. Every person in your group, physically able, will contribute if asked for the right contribution. Define the need, and fill the spot. All have talents, some just hide them better than others. To find those talents and get them into the light of day is not an easy task, but seldom will you be turned down when you can describe exactly the task that needs to be done. ASK!

PROFILE OF A GENEALOGICAL STUDENT

"Anyone who stops learning is old, whether at twenty or eighty. Anyone who keeps learning stays young. The greatest thing in life is to keep your mind young." --- Henry Ford.

Adult Education Principle: Adults learn what they want to learn. This may seem obvious, but it is surprising how often this fact is ignored. Adult education has no pre-requisite--educationally. I have had students with an 8th grade education in the same class with Ph. D.'s. It seems to make absolutely no difference. All one needs to know is how to read and write. These students are there for one reason only -- TO LEARN HOW TO DO THEIR OWN GENEALOGY!

Genealogical students are different from most other students. They are eager, energetic, bright and enthusiastic. They want to know everything -- NOW! They have one major theme in mind, genealogy. They are there to learn how to do their OWN genealogy.

These students are usually very patient in a classroom situation. They are willing to listen, although they may already "know" that particular aspect of the subject, just in case there is one item that may trigger their thoughts for their own research.

Genealogy students are usually older and more insistent on explanations. They will expect your material to be relevant to the subject. There are exceptions to all of the above, of course. I have taught many courses to both grade and high school levels, to scout troops and camps, but that is a different teaching technique.

The adult student has come to the learning market voluntarily and he expects value. He is more concerned with learning than the average student in other fields. You will not find a student enrolled in these classes who is uninterested.

Remembering the average age of your class will let you overlook the occasional nodding or closed eye. This does not mean you are boring -- its just a fact of life. Consider the time slot you were given. A genealogy class is seldom given 9 a.m. classes by an educational institution. Those are reserved for full-time students. You may be permitted the use of rooms in an afternoon when full-time student classes are not as numerous.

Other students in your class may be full of energy, alert and show tremendous ability to learn. Understanding may be sharper and retention greater than the average student. They may be a bit slower at taking notes and may need handouts for multi-paged material, but do not misjudge their ability to grasp the most difficult of concepts.

A student assignment was to abstract any newspaper articles concerning his family and to place the material on family group sheets. One student, who did not have newspaper accounts about her own family, turned in the following:

> MARK TWAIN, as a cub reporter, was told to NEVER state as fact anything that he could not personally verify. Following this instruction to the letter he wrote the following account of a local social event:
>
> "A woman giving the name of Mrs. James Jones, who is reported to be one of the social leaders of the city, is said to have given what was purported to be a party yesterday to a number of alleged ladies. The hostess claims to be the wife of a reputed attorney."

Adult students are more concerned with learning, on the whole, than younger students, so do not treat them with condescension. Assume that all your students are serious and you will not be disappointed.

The one thing this author has not had to address has been discipline problems. Instead, expect strong support from these students. They are quick to praise, eager to learn, thus easing the burden of keeping the interest level high. Adult genealogical students usually do NOT NEED TO BE MOTIVATED. They come to class with a high "built-in" interest factor.

PROFILE OF A GENEALOGICAL TEACHER

Should I become a teacher, or a writer? If you must ask that question, select teaching. If you have able pupils, you will learn. There is no greater satisfaction in life than to keep growing.

Everyone of us doing any kind of genealogy is a teacher to someone. Whether we have the "name tag" teacher or not, we are teachers. If you are conversing at a genealogical meeting, you are teaching! If you are exchanging information by mail, you are teaching! If you are talking on the telephone about genealogy, you are teaching! And the list goes on.

Stand back at your next genealogical meeting and listen. Every little group is talking about genealogy! Not politics, nor illness, nor any other subject -- but talking about genealogy. Each person is listening just long enough to hear the speaker catch a breath so he can get in his own family research "finds" or problems. Listen to the lilt in the voice of someone who has just made a "breakthrough" of a difficult problem. We are each teachers of a subject that is dear to our hearts. We all need to develop habits of listening to what other researchers have to say about how they found success. We need to cultivate open-mindedness.

In a field that is self-oriented by nature, the genealogical teacher gives of himself. I have never known a teacher of this subject who went into the field for money. We all start by giving of our time and effort because of our love of genealogy.

Our field is too broad for any ONE person to know everything about each phase of the subject. However, it is an excellent opportunity for CONTINUING or ADULT EDUCATION.

A teacher who takes the time and trouble to gear lessons toward the students will be asked to teach again. If you are now teaching, you owe it to your students to know all you can learn and to keep learning. A teacher who "knows it all," will miss many details which do not fall into preconceived patterns; patterns of possible poor research practices which compound problems.

No one person can continue to be "the teacher" within a group. No matter how small that group is, it will soon need some outside help. This author had been the only teacher for a group for almost ten years before it became clear that there were others who had become teacher material -- second generation, so to speak. And as in our own second generation, biologically, we all are aware that our children know more than we do, thus these second generation pupils were/are very knowledgeable. Reluctant as they were, and you are, you are teacher material. You may be saying now, "Mary fits all those qualifications. She would make a good teacher." And she is saying the same thing about you. Have you thought about teaching?

Do you need to know that someone else is there that you "think" could answer all those questions? NO ONE CAN ANSWER ALL THE QUESTIONS. As a teacher, all we can say or do is honestly reply, "I don't know, but let's see where we can find that answer," and follow through. Write it down so you can look it up later. NEVER leave a student hanging. At least TRY to find that answer or give them direction.

Some students have a tendency to dominate a session with their own personal genealogy. As a teacher, I've used a little bit of doggerel to get back on track such as:

"I can trace MY ancestry back to a protoplasmal, primordial, atomic globule. Consequently, my family pride is something inconceivable. I can't help it, I was born sneering!"

EDUCATIONAL QUALIFICATIONS FOR A GENEALOGY TEACHER---EXPERIENCE: Not in teaching, but in the field of research and the willingness to put forth the effort to study a book on "How-to" practices for basic/beginning genealogy. Even if you are an experienced researcher, these books give ideas for where to start teaching. If you understand the basic principles in a step-by-step manner, you can teach.

There are higher education courses offered at many major educational facilities which offer accreditation in the field of genealogy. Until these graduates get into the field in all areas of the country, and other institutions begin offering the courses for credit, those of us who do not have those degrees will learn to do with what we have.

The main qualifications for a teacher at the local level are THE NEED AND THE DESIRE. Your basic knowledge can and will be of great value. These qualifications will be what is needed for the teacher of genealogy. Simply stated, A TEACHER IS ONE WHO GIVES OF HIMSELF. That person must be patient and caring. These are the ONLY true qualifications for teaching our favorite subject.

OVERVIEW OF GENEALOGICAL EDUCATION

Colleges and universities all over the world are now offering degrees for credit, and individual courses both credit and non-credit, in the field of GENEALOGY. We are grateful for these courses. This book is not attempting to direct the focus on this field. It is intended to be a practical work, targeted at the local society member using all the sources and resources that are available to teach genealogy as a non-credit course.

Genealogical education needs to be viewed differently from that of general education. It is not structured as the educational system of kindergarten through grade 12. Since there has been no structure drawn in the field, there seems to be at least two separate and distinct feelings toward the structuring of teaching. Those two fields of thought are:

1. There are three classes of genealogy - Basic/Beginning, Intermediate and Advanced.

2. There are no categories, just periods of time involved in the field of research. That genealogy is based on the basic/beginning skills taught first, then expanded, as a topic.

When we acknowledge that we are continuing to learn no matter how long we have been diligently researching, we admit to ourselves that basically the word ADVANCED may not fit our own acceptance of our own research skills. Perhaps we may have been working for years and never had the advantage of a basic course. If these facts apply, would we be embarrassed to take a basic course? Who are we to presume that we could teach? Past educational background need not be a pre-requisite.

As long as the skills that we have used are good basic skills, we should have no insurmountable problems, either in our own research or in teaching at any level. Everything genealogically is based on these basic/beginning classes.

Some of the basic skills of teaching, as well as learning, are based on the educational system's basic skills. One may want to investigate some refresher courses; courses to audit or for credit. Maybe a basic class on library science or study skills may open your eyes and mind to a lot of things that have been escaping you.

Another idea might be to collect shelf lists of nearby libraries' genealogical holdings, AGLL (American Genealogical Lending Library) catalogs, NGS (National Genealogical Society) lending library lists, or any lending institution lists that make available to you and your students the materials needed. I, personally, use catalogs as a source to let me know what books are available for sale. If they are available for sale, they are available on interlibrary loan. Even small libraries have collections that are usable to the genealogical teacher; materials such as directories, atlases, newspapers and such materials that are not in a "genealogical" department. The idea is to have that resource material in mind and to know where to find it.

To keep current in the field, one must read-read-read all current publications, newsletters, journals, etc. Many organizations are offering courses by mail or seminar form (see next). The newest educational form is the VIDEO TAPE. Currently, there are none that are very professional in film quality, but they are great on content. The cost is as low as $8.00 per film rental. The content of these films is a great source for the small group for educational purposes, and an untapped source for the teacher. MATERIAL may be gleaned while watching one or more of the "experts" in their presentation.

Audio tapes are available on the same basis, usually for purchase. These are sold by various organizations for approximately $5.00. THE FEDERATION OF GENEALOGICAL SOCIETIES (See Bibliography for address) tapes all of the sessions (over 100) each year at their conference to sell as a service to people just like us.

SOME PROGRAMS CURRENTLY BEING OFFERED ON A CONTINUING EDUCATION BASIS THROUGHOUT THE COUNTRY

National Genealogical Society
Home Study Program: American Genealogy
A Basic Course Educational Division, Department N.
1921 Sunderland Pl. N. W.
Washington, D.C. 20306
Currently graduating approximately 150 students per year. Also seminars on Genealogical Education & Instructor Development Committees.

Institute of Genealogy & Historical Research
Co-Sponsored by the Board of Certification of Genealogists
Samford University Library
Birmingham, AL 35229
Annual since 1988 - One-Week Courses.

National Institute on Genealogical Research
P. O. Box 14727
Washington D.C. 20044-7274
and
National Archives Educational Branch
Co-Sponsors Institutes Annually.

Brigham Young University
136 Harmon Building
Provo, UT 84602
Accredited Courses, Institutes, Degrees.

Federation of Genealogical Societies
P. O. Box 220
Davenport, IA 52805
Annual Conference/Tapes/Speakers' Lists/Etc.

Heritage Quest
P. O. Box 40
Orting, WA 98360-0040
Road Tours/Seminars/Annual Research Tours/Magazines/Supplies/Books/Audio Tapes/Video Tapes/Publisher/Printer.

Everton Publishers
3223 South Main Street
Nibley, UT 84321
Journal/Supplies/Publisher

CHOOSING A CURRICULUM

COURSES? WHAT COURSES? TAUGHT WHEN? WHAT DO WE OFFER OUR MEMBERS? All questions that arise when discussing teaching genealogy.

Basic/beginning genealogy should be taught on a regular basis. These classes will continue the growth of our organizations. But beyond that, what else? That question is difficult to answer with a simple --- "Whatever your group needs." But who is to say what the needs are? Anything after beginning classes should be in order of need.

Defining the need may be the biggest problem you face. Have there been requests voiced with officers of your group (or even hints)? Have there been requests at your local continuing education facility (have you asked)? Are there requests at your local Chamber of Commerce? Many times these requests are not reported to the Society. Unless you ask, you may never hear from them. If there has been one request, you can bet there are others out there searching for what you have to offer.

Probably the most frequently used method of defining the need is to pass around at your meetings options of titles of classes (titles and topics may be found at the end of this chapter). Or even a blank sheet of paper requesting areas of research may be passed around, although this method leaves a great deal to be desired because often it does not produce specifics; whereas the topic form asking for a check beside the topic desired brings immediate results. CAUTION; Do not present too many titles or topics at one time.

It is not necessary to have a teacher in mind when the topic/title page is passed. The teacher may not live in the immediate vicinity. He may be recruited from another area, or even another field of research. If county court records are on the title list, you may consider a member as teacher, with recruited help from the county clerk's office.

The teacher need not be an "expert in the field". A few years ago I asked, by a show of hands, how many would be interested in a class on New York research. Twelve hands were raised from a group of eighty. The course was researched, outlined and designed. The outline appeared in our small, 12-page quarterly. The class was announced in the Community College Catalog. Twenty-seven students enrolled and seventeen letters from throughout the country were received. People who had seen the outline (on our exchange program) were requesting materials. All this from a group of less than two hundred membership, and from a teacher who had never had personal or professional experience in the State of New York.

When thinking of expansion or sequel courses (those offered after basic/beginning), consider the following: Most teachers seem to try to cover a great deal of material in this first course, and they should. It may be the only class some of the students ever take. Should or could these subjects be expanded into "in-depth" courses, based on the basic knowledge? Take county court records, which are taught in the basic/beginning course. There is enough material available to teach a course called "County Court Records" for a semester, or at least an for extended class. In sequence courses, review the basic/beginning outline. See what subjects there could be expanded and taught in depth.

Although the teacher may be THE most knowledgeable person on SWEDISH (or any other subject), genealogy in your Society, unless the students have NEED for SWEDISH genealogy, they will not listen. Nor will they have need to listen. Keep in mind that THE STUDENT'S NEEDS SHOULD BE THE FIRST CONSIDERATION.

CONSIDERATIONS FOR CHOOSING A CURRICULUM

FIRST: A curriculum should not be prepackaged or too rigid. It should be flexible and geared to the unique needs of students.

SECOND: A curriculum should start from an "experience" base. Experience of the students coupled with that of the teacher's knowledge.

THIRD: A curriculum should be oriented toward the present -- to what is available to study in the present -- to materials available to both student and teacher with a minimum of effort.

FOURTH: A curriculum should emphasize WHY, WHAT and WHERE.

FIFTH: A curriculum should be based on reality of time, place and teacher availability. We can adjust our sights and lower our wishes on all but the quality of teaching. The hardware of teaching (time, place and equipment) may be adjusted, but not the quality of teaching.

SAMPLE TOPICS AND TITLES

The following list of topics and titles are samples suggested for classes, seminars, workshops, etc. You will note that some of these titles are "cute," but these often bring in people who would otherwise not be intrigued by a common title. Also note that some are excellent topics for a speaker at a meeting when only one hour or less is available. Others are, by their nature, a full semester or prolonged course. The topic or title may make or break a course, so choose your topic carefully. There are hundreds of ideas. The following are only a few. Why not design your own?

- Vital Records and Their Substitutes
- Probate Records
- County Court Records
- Town Records
- Evidence
- Land and Deed Records
- Handwriting
- Letter Writing
- Home Sources
- Maps
- Adoptees
- War Records
- Terminology
- Analyzation
- Newspapers
- Census
  - Federal
  - State
  - Special
  - Soundex
  - Miracode
- Libraries
- Computers
- Mormon Records
- Ethics in Genealogy
- Blood Lines Vs. Ink Lines
- Where Do I Go Next?
- Finding Maiden Names
- Immigration
- Naturalization
- Migration
- Church Records
- Institution Records
- Countries (By Name)
- Ethnic Groups (By Name)
- Primary Evidence Vs. Secondary Evidence
- Preservation
- Family Traditions
- When To Use A Professional
- Area Research, United States
  - Southern
  - New England
  - Mid-Atlantic
- Interlibrary Loan

Publishing
Problem Solving
Passenger Lists
Oral History
Lineage Societies
Atlases, Gazetteers
County Histories
Note Keeping
Evaluation
Proof -- What Is It?
Kinship Terminology
Fraternal & Social Organizations
Business Records
Court Dockets
Ancient Printed Records
Charting
Numbering Systems
Filing Systems
Pending Suits
Judgments-Direct/Reverse
Soldier & Sailor Relief Records
Ministers' Licenses
Common Pleas
State Cases
Minute Books
Law Records
Decennial Reports
Case File Packets
Appearance Dockets
Chancery Records
Testamentary Records
Estrays
Ferry License Records
Sheriff's Summonses
The Fallibility of Indexes
Geographic Titles Such As:
Hudson & Mohawk Valleys
Borden's Grant
Penn's Grant
South of the Green River
Quakers/All Areas
Ethnic & Religious Groups
Library of Congress Catalogs
Down East Ancestors
Consider Collaterals
Principles of Genealogical Evidence
Reconstruction of Property Holdings
Courthouse Burned?
National Union Catalog of Manuscript Collections
Church Records
Coping With Common Surnames
Alphabet Soup
The Dark Ages
Preponderance of Evidence

TEACHER'S PLANNING

Planning is the most important step you can take. It is important to plan ahead on any endeavor you undertake whether it be your own research field or in the teaching field.

By nature, the genealogy teacher has the basic skills in specific fields of research and will not usually be asked to teach in areas of which he knows little or nothing. There are, however, exceptions.

EXCEPTION EXAMPLE:

Recently a number of students asked for a class on Tennessee. Applying the basic rules of general research and outlining the problems, I began building a class based on general genealogical skills. Searching for specifics, this planning took some time because of my unfamiliarity with the State of Tennessee's materials. Materials were gathered (actually a large box of materials), reviewed and placed in eight file folders for there were eight periods in which to teach the class. These folders were labeled as to content. The outline was evident in the folder titles.
(End of Example)

In many instances, your planning may be done by defining a need. If you are a beginning/basic teacher, many good books are available to start a class outline. (See BIBLIOGRAPHY) Often the book title and table of contents will provide you with an automatic outline. A SAMPLE course outline is included in this section later.

When planning has begun, always remember to review your time slot, that time allotted for you to teach, then the subject and then the material.

Materials are chosen by personal choice. Be comfortable with your choice and it will show in your teaching.

The TITLE of your course should be chosen before the planning stage begins. Gathering materials without a title may result in mass confusion. You, the teacher, may be asked to choose the topic.

STEPS TO BE TAKEN IN YOUR PLANNING FOR A CLASS (Not necessarily in this order.)

1. Review materials available to YOU AND YOUR STUDENTS.

A. If you have a small genealogical collection available locally, you might want to review catalogs, lending library, interlibrary loan, printed bibliographies, etc., for their availability.

B. Check your own personal library; not necessarily books, but materials indexed and cataloged so carefully by you at the time you were doing your research.

2. Check some of the standard books on the market such as:

"THE SOURCE, A GUIDEBOOK OF AMERICAN GENEALOGY," edited by Arlene Eakle and Johni Cerny; published by Ancestry Publishing Company, Salt Lake City, Utah. 1984.

"BUILDING AN AMERICAN PEDIGREE," by Norman Wright; published by B.Y.U. University Press.

(Any other similar book, see BIBLIOGRAPHY.)

The material in these books, or similar books, have more than enough information for a full course on almost any subject or title that you might choose. CHECK EACH INDEX (there is more than meets the eye), the material is there for you. It is your responsibility to dig it out. The same material is available for your students, but they want to be SPOON-FED.

3. Review the notes, handouts, and photocopies of materials that you gleaned in your own research. A personal story, used as an example, is always easier to understand and it is also easier for the teacher to use an example with which he is most familiar.

4. OUTLINE YOUR COURSE: From the materials gathered, a pattern will form for your outline. The materials will fall into several categories. This becomes your outline. (See sample OUTLINE at end of chapter.)

5. CHECK LIST: There are many check lists available for the teacher. Two examples are:

PREPARATION CHECK LIST

A. Acquiring knowledge as thoroughly as possible of the topic being taught.

B. Checking to make certain sufficient material is available for both teacher and student.

C. Check room facilities and materials to be used within that classroom by the teacher. (Audiovisual Aids - See Audiovisual Chapter.)

D. Outline the course.

E. Prepare file cards, note cards, audiovisual materials, handouts, etc. for classroom presentation.

PLANNING CHECK LIST

HAVE YOU:

Outlined your objectives?
Analyzed your students needs?
Arranged for administrative details to be handled through co-sponsoring affiliation?
(Local Continuing Education Department, Etc.)

A class is only as good as its teacher. The teacher is only as good as the preparations made for conducting the class. Preparation by the teacher is the most important step to be taken to build confidence in ability to teach a rewarding class.

OUTLINING your course may seem simple, and it is! Do it once, and the skill is yours for life. It is nothing more than an overview of material using key words or phrases and designing a plan to follow. An agenda designing to help you keep on track and help you remember points necessary to stay within the outline and the time period that you have to teach.

The basic/beginning course could not be taught without using forms and charts. No one can travel in unfamiliar territory without a road map without getting lost. Family group sheets and pedigree charts are your sign posts. The outline for your classes is your road map; it keeps you from getting lost.

Any outline you design is not "set in concrete." It is not rigid or unbending. It can be changed at any time. It is a simple written idea of where you are going.

SAMPLE BASIC
BEGINNING OUTLINE

I. **GETTING STARTED RIGHT**

   A. Home Survey
   B. Interviewing
   C. Charting

II. **ORGANIZATION**

   A. Filing System
   B. Learning NEVER to repeat
   C. Forms - Why and How

III. **VITAL RECORDS**

   A. Birth, Marriage & Death - Where and How
   B. Reconstruction of same

IV. **CENSUS RECORDS**

   A. 1790-1910 Federal
   B. State

V. **THE INDEX APPROACH**

   A. Survey of work done by others

VI. **STATE & FEDERAL RECORDS**

   A. State Archives
   B. Federal Archives
   C. Regional Archives

VII. **COUNTY AND PARISH RECORDS**

   A. Probate
   B. Land and Deed records
   C. Tax Records

VIII. **REVIEW AND QUESTIONS**

SAMPLE OUTLINE

MIGRATION, IMMIGRATION AND NATURALIZATION

I. **OVERVIEW, IMMIGRATION & EMIGRATION**

A. Trends Over Time
B. Motivation

II. **PATTERNS OF GROUP MIGRATION**

A. Puritans, Huguenots, German, Irish, Scots, Palatines, Pilgrims, Quakers, etc.

III. **PREPARATION FOR THE VOYAGE**

A. Meeting Physical Needs
B. Documents, Records
C. The Role of Brokers (Companies)
D. Immigrant Aid Societies
E. Records Left In Country of Debarkation
F. Indentures There and Here

IV. **THE VOYAGE**

A. Organizations
B. Manifests
C. Customs
D. Vital Records On-Board Ship

V. **ARRIVAL**

A. Pest Hospitals
B. Newspapers
C. Ellis Islands Throughout the Country
D. Companies' Responsibilities
E. Orphan Trains
F. Passenger Lists
G. Denizens

VI. **NATURALIZATION**

A. Early-Pre-1776
B. Chronological 1776-1906
C. Americanization of Surnames

VII. **THE TRIP INLAND**

A. Oaths of Allegiance
B. Migration Patterns

VIII. **NATURALIZATION PROCESS**

A. All Records Chronologically
B. Sources:
    a. National
    b. State
    c. County/Town

ORGANIZATION OF MATERIALS

The materials used for teaching come from many sources. Often you may use information directly from a specific text of your choice. There are many from which to choose. (For a few ideas for making those choices see BIBLIOGRAPHY included later.) When using these texts, review their chapter headings or outlines.

In working from your own accumulation of materials and trying to define the direction in which you should go, you may want to review those chapter headings to see how authors have divided their materials. The suggestion for designing your own is LOGIC. Logic, in that it makes sense when presented in a certain form for you and your students to follow. You cannot get too far afield since nothing seems to be out of order in the learning or the teaching process. There are few books that give an exact STEP-BY-STEP process for learning or teaching.

The materials you have in your own files may not be in a sequence to present to a class. If your organizational skills are GREAT, teach your own method of organization. Most people do not admit to having organizational skills, although they do. However, if you are really unorganized, begin with creating some order out of your own chaos, otherwise your disorganized skills will come through to your students.

Genealogical materials are either organized by TIME-FRAME or geographically. No matter what the material, it will answer the question of what, where, when or how. If your material falls into these categories, begin by placing them under these headings. This will soon form your outline.

EXAMPLE: CLASS ON BIRTH RECORDS

WHAT: Birth Records
WHEN: By Time Frame
1906 to today (V R by State)
1888 to 1906 (By County/Town, etc)
1850 to 1888 (Scattered)
Pre -- 1850 (By Locality)
HOW: Printed Records, Bible Records, Archives, County Histories, Printed Vital Statistics By Town, W.P.A. Indexes, etc.

WHY: When all else fails, finding substitutes for vital records.

Your outline will form your organizational skills and put your ideas on paper. The materials will place themselves into categories for filing and easy retrieval. Organization and planning go hand in hand. The materials used in the teaching situation must be organized and planned. The skills learned in these processes will help you in teaching and in your own personal research.

METHODOLOGY

The form used to convey the message of Genealogy is called methodology. The methods available to all, wherever one lives, are the same. The TERMINOLOGY is most different. One kind of class may be taught as a "workshop" in one area, while in another area it may be called a "class." Reference to the types of methods used in teaching will differ from locality to locality. There seems to be a difference in terminology and not in content. Thus the following is a list of CURRENT TERMINOLOGY. There is no need to change YOUR vocabulary to suit the following. The content alone will be of help in choosing a method to teach genealogy. Each will be defined and described in detail in the following sections.

1. LECTURE
2. DISCUSSION-QUESTIONS
3. CASE STUDIES
4. ROLE PLAYING
5. PROGRAM
6. PROJECT
7. WORKSHOP
8. STUDY GROUPS
9. FAIRS
10. CARAVAN/TOUR
11. LIBRARY TOUR
12. CLASS OR COURSE
13. CONVERSATION
14. CONFERENCE/SEMINAR

LECTURE

As a method of teaching genealogy, the educational system relies on the LECTURE plus laboratory work as their main methodology. Through the lecture information is given and specific principles are taught. Applying these principles, the laboratory would be our own study area at home and the research facilities available to us. The lecture is pre-prepared and differs from other forms of methodology in that the lecturer (speaker) is given a specific time period in which to disseminate materials. There may be time given at the end of the lecture for questions.

In preparing for the lecture, as with all other forms of education, the outline is most necessary. Keeping notes handy, even when the material is extremely familiar, helps to keep us "on track."

The lecture method is interchangeable with several other methods such as program, class, etc.

QUESTIONS

Discussion, that art of interpersonal communication between two people to get a point across, is a form of teaching that COULD be considered a program.

Two or more people conversing is a discussion. A discussion in a large group may involve many people. Large group discussions are hard to manage and that silent, shy person is often left out.

THERE ARE NO DUMB QUESTIONS in genealogy. I begin each class with this statement, put the students at ease and encourage questions.

Explain your personal rules. If you prefer not to be interrupted during a session, state that there will be time for questions later.

Class discussion is usually motivated by questions. Discussion is most important for the teacher for here is where ideas are formed and you learn about your students' needs. Guiding genealogical discussion can be rewarding. Asking or answering questions with questions is one method of teaching.

Specific lineage questions are, of course, hard to answer because they are so very personal, but even those questions should be encouraged. A training period, defining how to word specific questions to make them more general may be in order. Teaching how to redesign questions to make them general may take some thought. A five-minute dissertation on great-grandfather may be condensed into one question.

> EXAMPLE: I am searching for the birth date of John JONES. He was in LYNCHBURG, Virginia in 1824 paying taxes for the first time on one adult male and one horse. Where do I look next?

This short question, gleaned from a five-minute talk from a student and shortened, may be a way to teach more direct questioning. (The answer may be to "guess" that John was probably 21 in 1824, paying taxes for the first time, and that a starting time-frame might be 1803.)

ANSWERS

Do your students expect answers? Yes, but NO TEACHER KNOWS ALL THE ANSWERS. NO TEACHER IS EXPECTED TO KNOW ALL THE ANSWERS. All he can be expected to know are the resources to help find those answers. The many books, pamphlets and articles studied give clues to help find those answers.

Answering questions with questions is a teaching method which makes the students think! Part of our responsibility is to create an investigative mind. Change words around and redirect questions. "Yes" and "No" answered questions do not work well with this method. In redirecting questions ask: who? what? when? why? where? and how? If any of these can be inserted at the beginning of the question, it can be redirected.

> EXAMPLE: "Jane. HOW would you answer that?" Or, "Jane. WHAT do you think Millie should do to unravel this problem?"

The value of the direct question is to help draw out those people who are sometimes timid or reluctant to state opinions. Experience shows that a person who takes part in a class, contributes to that class, and the contribution makes him feel a real PART of that class.

CASE STUDIES

There are printed articles and parts of books that deal with the use of case studies as a genealogical teaching method. (See the BIBLIOGRAPHY chapter, or draw from your own research.) These may be "made up" cases but be careful with this. Some people have problems with dates and places with which they are not familiar.

Case studies are used to define or refine a point that has been taught. Studying a case with all its problems may bring out the many varied ways we go about solving specific problems. Students can often "see" a point when put into historical settings that may match their own research problems.

ROLE PLAYING

A little-used method of genealogical teaching is the theatrical reading or playing out a set of ideas with students taking a role and actually playing out that role in front of a class (or from their seats). The idea is to make them think, or visualize, their own ancestor in a particular role. Roles are assigned to each student, such as the roles of John Smith, his wife, his brother-in-law, father-in-law, uncle, niece, a neighbor... Note the various relationships and different surnames. This becomes very important.

The teacher sets the scene, which can change continually to include various events and times. Two examples of time and place may be 1824, big city, eastern state, family discussing migration to Ohio; or pre-1860, mid Missouri, discussing leaving for Texas. Any scene can be used that creates a situation to make the student THINK of what actually affected their ancestor. The role playing puts them in that position of creating dialogue about what our ancestors actually talked about. It also involves a large portion of the class in varying degrees of input. It can be, and usually is, FUN!

PROGRAM

The program is the more structured method of teaching. It is identified and defined by the society with a specific time and place, on a regular basis. It is probably the most important aspect of all teaching methods because it may be the only education some students ever receive. The speaker (or lecturer) is asked, for this one time engagement, to impart knowledge on a specific subject. The speakers need not necessarily be genealogists.

EXAMPLES:
An archivist speaking on preservation.
A county clerk on courthouse records
A lawyer on probate records.
A church official on church records.
A parks and recreation official on battlefields
A librarian on interlibrary loan.

The possibilities are endless. The general idea is that the program is teaching an aspect of genealogy to the largest group available to a local genealogical organization.

Generally, the subject of a program should be chosen before the speaker is obtained. This is not always the way it is done, but it CAN work. At least give your speaker a general idea of a topic.

We all need historical background from which to base our research, but there are historical societies for just this kind of program.

PROJECTS

Projects are designed to further restoration and preservation of old records. It is a teaching method that might be related to the laboratory setting.

When we transcribe tombstones, we learn what is in an old cemetery and can apply that knowledge to the locality of our personal research. When we transcribe marriage, birth or death records, the same applies. The project is a learning tool as well as a service project.

Project ideas and their implementation are another avenue of growth. They provide a learning situation. More importantly, they provide an avenue to gather materials together as a unit with a theme. They involve people working on a specific theme, the project. Involvement of many people make for an active society, and an active society brings membership growth.

WORKSHOPS

Workshop, as a word, is the most confusing educational word in the field. It seems to mean different things in different parts of the country. A workshop usually means a group of people who gather together on a regular basis to study a specific topic, usually with a leader, but not always. Sometimes these workshops are held for a short period, one to two hours, with a leader directing a group discussion or presenting material on a pre-announced subject. It can also mean a leader on hand to help at a research center for a specified time, meeting at a home or public room, bringing your own materials (well-marked, of course) and sharing with others; or working in the home of a member who has a collection of notes on a specific area, who has graciously opened his/her home on occasion for research purposes.

The large general workshop may mean a day with many teachers in various rooms, teaching classes on varied subjects from which the student must choose few classes because of time limitations.

WORKSHOPS are various forms of teaching and learning. The word can mean almost anything you want it to mean.

STUDY GROUPS

A group of students interested in a certain aspect of genealogy who get together to work toward a specific goal, or study a specific topic, form a study group. These groups do not always have just one teacher. One person may be responsible for each different phase of a subject. The study group is usually loosely organized. It uses the knowledge of many teachers, although if called teachers, they would be surprised at the label; but, they are teachers. The learning in these groups is delightful. It is a period of enjoyment. Small tips learned here can be found in few other learning situations. Study groups use methods that have little or no structure, but do create lots of learning.

FAIRS

Genealogy FAIRS are a comparatively new name as a form or method of education. They seem to be "fun" oriented but the educational aspect is always there. Fairs may be places to sell or display items as money-making projects, and include speakers/lectures/program/etc. The name FAIR may be substituted for SEMINAR/CONFERENCE/WORKSHOP/or others.

CARAVANS OR TOURS

Another idea becoming popular, because of the fabulous research centers throughout the world and bargain rates of transportation, is the caravan or tour, a group of people traveling together for genealogical education and research purposes. A director may teach or direct, as the title implies. Travel time and accommodation time may be used as teaching periods. The time may be spent in describing where you are going and what you can expect to find in these facilities. It is a great time to share ideas.

LIBRARY TOURS

Basically, Library Tours are the same as Caravan or Tour except we do not think in terms of long distance. We, as researchers, seem to think that each new library we visit may have that "certain" clue which will be a breakthrough and give us all our answers. We travel, usually in small groups, to visit each collection that is within driving distance. The educational part of this continues during the trip to and from, and during lunch. Be sure to LISTEN to these intense conversations with fellow traveling companions.

CLASSES OR COURSES

A course is defined as a series of instructional periods dealing with genealogy. The course provides the instruction and the students enrolled in the course are "taking" the class for a specified period of time; a semester is six or eight weeks of intense eight-hour days. The classroom situation is the most formal of all educational methods and commands the most respect from the public and the genealogical community. Methods of teaching a class are outlined in this book to present ideas and inspiration.

CONVERSATIONS

That buzzzz that you hear at your meeting is called CONVERSATION. It is a teaching and learning method. Stop and listen, really listen, at your next meeting. The conversation you hear is strictly about genealogy. This phenomenon means you hear nothing else except genealogy. Most people do not listen except for that pause which means that they can jump in and talk about their own research. As a teacher, LISTEN. You will hear the problems of research that need to be addressed. LISTEN.

CONFERENCES/SEMINARS

The Conference/Seminar involves many people in the decision-making, not always the individual teacher. It is included here because we, as teachers, are often asked to "do" or help organize a seminar. The ideas here are to help you in that organization but not necessarily in how to teach in the conference/seminar situation.

The educational method of teaching which uses the Conference/Seminar form is probably the most widely used. The two terms seem interchangeable in their meaning. The definition of the terms are long and varied with the theme of education being foremost in that meaning. They are:

1. A pooling of knowledge/experience and opinions among a group of people.

2. The act of consulting together formally.

3. A planned meeting for learning one subject.

4. A designed program to promote constructive thinking.

5. A designed program to motivate.

6. Planned programs to increase membership.

7. Designed programs to involve members, friends and guests from farther distances as well as members who live locally.

Notice, many of the above statements involve the words designed and planned in their statements.

The Conference/Seminar (hereafter referred to as seminar) is pre-thought out and planned/designed for a specific purpose. The better planned, the better the seminar.

The seminar planning committee personnel, elected or appointed, should be in place at least one year prior to the seminar. This may seem like a long time, especially for the first one attempted, but it takes a lot of time for proper planning. A sample outline might include some of the following:

PLANNING A SEMINAR -- OUTLINE

OBJECTIVE -
Outline what you need and what you want to accomplish. This should be your first step.

PARTICIPANTS -
Target your participants for your seminar. Your own members only? Guests? Local Community? Other lineage societies? Expanded community? Those living some distance away? Identifying your participants as a beginning step will help answer questions later.

TEACHERS, SPEAKERS -
Early in the planning stages, ask yourself some of the following "SHOULD WE?" questions.

A. Make use of local talent? To what extent? All or part?

B. Take advantage of some of the "businesses" currently touring the country such as Heritage Quest, Everton Publishers or others in the field? (See BIBLIOGRAPHY for addresses.) If the answer is "yes" to this question, you need to get on the schedule early.

C. Use state or expanded community-recognized speakers about whom a great deal is known?

D. Ask for a speakers list from some of the groups which provide such a list? Does your state organization provide such a list? The FEDERATION OF GENEALOGICAL SOCIETIES provides such a list and is available to you. (For address, see BIBLIOGRAPHY.)

E. Use a nationally known "Name" speaker?

FACILITIES -

Investigate places available and create a list of their offerings. The capacity, price, physical plant, time availability (time may affect price), and suitability. Every community, no matter what size, has meeting facilities such as church, building and loan associations, banks, libraries, educational facilities, etc. The list is endless. It is the responsibility of the planning committee to consider all possibilities, remembering accommodations both for guests and speakers, and to make the decisions early.

Check hotel/motels. If you use their food service, they often have facilities free of charge. They expect confirmed reservations at least one week in advance and the sponsoring group is responsible for all reservations. They usually give a ten percent break on "no-shows."

Educational facilities are available. Check for vacation time, break time, the times not used by students. Local school boards are most receptive. The key is to convince them you are an EDUCATIONALLY-ORIENTED GROUP. Some pitfalls! Watch those chairs, especially elementary class chairs which are not built for adult bodies!

Attempting to determine the number of people that can be expected is tough, at least for the first endeavor. Try using the average number of people attending your local meetings, add thirty people and begin with that number. Your guess will be as good as any other. After your first endeavor, you will have a more stable base from which to work. In all things you do, you must grow. To grow, your reputation of putting on a "good" program will be most important for this growth period.

PRICE -

Price is a difficult subject to address because of the many variables. Does your society need to earn money for a project? If not, the first seminar maybe should be planned as a "break-even" seminar. The example here would be exactly what you do with your household budget. Get it down on paper, figure all costs, and with these figures in front of you add ten percent to cover the unexpected expenses. Be extremely careful of CHARGES. Most PUBLIC buildings, by law, cannot permit charging admission. A donation may not cover your expenses.

MATERIALS, EQUIPMENT, HANDOUTS, AUDIOVISUAL AIDS, PRINTING COSTS, THE HARDWARE OF A SEMINAR -

The equipment required for teaching should be specified by your teachers. All should be contacted well in advance to consider their needs. You will not know what they need unless you ask. Ask them to choose a satisfactory date. Pre-arrangement of expenses will eliminate unexpected surprises. Printed programs are nice, but not necessarily a must unless this seminar is in many segments. If this is so, then the participants need to know where to go, when, or even what choices to make. An outline of your program in print is one of the items that make your seminar appear more professional. Fortunately, as machines are perfected, printing is becoming less expensive.

Some businesses will permit their office machines for copying as a community service project. They may give permission for you to do your printing on their machines. Have you asked?

ADVERTISING -

Planning ahead on advertising is a must. Early advertising will increase your rate of success. Press release designs and copies of mailing lists take time to assemble. Various publications need to be notified early to assure best coverage. National publications in the field will advertise for you early if notified three to six months in advance.

Local Press Release: Advise them of a special interest speaker for an article. Human interest stories can be written early and scheduled for later release. Paid advertising should at least be considered. The rates for an educational enterprise that would benefit the community may have a very low rate in your area. ASK!

Radio and television coverage is fairly easy to acquire, if notified early. In interviewing guest speakers, ask them for their permission and their availability. If arriving from a distance, an interview may be set up early in the morning for airing later in the day. Speakers are usually glad to furnish you with a printed press release.

LOGISTICS -

The rooms needed, their availability and accessibility, restrooms, signs and all kinds of questions arise about the place you have chosen. Is the place easy to find? For you? For someone from out of town? If in doubt, consider signs. Consider permanent signs. They are an investment to be used from year to year. A simple sign with GENEALOGY and an arrow (each sign arrow pointing a different way) will be used from year to year. Signs tell our visitors where we are. Indoor signs point the way to various rooms, or registration, or restrooms, or whatever needs to be found.

Check room accessibility. Who is responsible for opening and closing doors. Nothing is more irritating than a class waiting to get into a locked room. I once held a class of eighty people outdoors in a drizzle because a room was locked.

CLEAN-UP COMMITTEE -

Is cleaning up the responsibility of a hard-working planning committee? The reputation of the genealogical community depends on everyone making the effort to leave the facility "better" than it was found. A most important work of the committee is that it works with public relations.

PRE-REGISTRATION AND REGISTRATION

Pre-registration by mail or phone will help to insure quicker starts at the time of the seminar. But we, as genealogists, are known for our procrastination. Do not expect one-hundred percent cooperation. Registration tables should be planned in advance. If you are expecting a large number of people, Review space needed and mentally place the tables considering the flow of people. You might use the alphabet system. Signs on the tables, "A" through "B" and "C" through "F", etc., will move people more quickly and efficiently.

If a payment is requested, then registration is necessary. If you are working with a donation, payment and registration may not be necessary. If your goal is to increase membership, a free seminar may be your target. A list passed with names and addresses to be signed will give you the contact with new people.

Please consider name tags. These may not seem important and may even seem an added nuisance and expense. But they are of value to everyone, especially those teachers who have other things on their minds. It may be embarrassing not to remember the name of the person you ate dinner with last night.

EVALUATION AND REPORT

We all need to know where to improve. If you started with no records, leave a set for the next committee. Keep records of what you have done. They will be appreciated as a base from which to work. A sample evaluation sheet is provided for a small seminar. Properly used, it can be of value in reviewing what has been accomplished and, also, what you did not do.

GENEALOGY SEMINAR QUESTIONNAIRE

Please fill out this questionnaire and return it to one of the teachers before you leave today. The information will help us plan future seminars better suited to your needs.

1. Is this your first seminar? Yes____ No____
2. I heard about the seminar At A Library____ Advertising ____ Other ____
3. Did the registration go quickly? Efficiently____
   Any suggestions for improvement?
4. The class periods were About Right____Too Short____ Too Long____ Other____
5. The routine of the seminar Ran Smoothly____ Needs improvement____ How____
6. Were the rooms easy to locate? Yes____ No____
7. Please evaluate your instructors:

PERIOD	INSTRUCTORS NAME	COMMENT
1.		
2.		
3.		
4.		
5.		

8. What classes would you like to attend at the next seminar?

____
____
____
____

9. In what areas of research are you most interested?

____
____
____
____

10. Would you attend another seminar here? Yes____ No____

OTHER COMMENTS:

____
____
____
____

THANKS FOR SHARING YOUR IDEAS!

PRESENTATION

We have discussed the profile of both the teacher and the student and are prepared to meet each student on an individual basis. The day has arrived when butterflies and nerves take over...the first day of class. You tell yourself all the negatives such as: "Don't drink too much or you'll have to go to the bathroom in the middle of class;" or, "I can't do this. Whatever possessed me to take this job?" These and similar thoughts have you in a cold sweat. THIS IS NORMAL! Most teachers go through this or something similar on a regular basis. Do not worry! Adjust your attitude and think positive. Things WILL work out. Here are just a few simple suggestions (nothing too difficult) on classroom presentation.

Pause at the door, swallow hard, stick out your chin and enter calmly. Your students are as apprehensive as you. A little laughter is great for a relaxed start. Introduce yourself. You may think everyone knows you, but don't take it for granted. Write the word GENEALOGY on the board. Spell it out, and the name of the course. Call the roll or have students introduce themselves. Get started in a relaxed manner.

Lay down your ground rules early. Let the students know who is in charge. You may need to state, "Thank you, Mrs. Jones, but we need to limit our time in order for others to have time to speak."

A feature of most classes is a sharing time when everyone tells where he or she is working in their own research. This is often done even in large gatherings but in the classroom it is an integral part of the whole. It is a relaxing time for the student, and a benefit for the teacher. It gives us clues as to which part of the very broad field of genealogy they will be needing to work on in this particular class. It is also a time for the teacher to relax.

PERSONAL APPEARANCE

DRESS:
The type of dress is relaxed, but professional. You are the expert -- the teacher of the day. Appearance counts. Be neat and clean. Your appearance will command respect.

PERSONAL BEARING-POSTURE:
Remember Mamma saying, "Stand up straight?" Do not slouch. If using a podium, do not lean on it. It is a place for your teaching materials. If you must be seated, keep erect. Make sure everyone can see you.

ATTITUDES:
Your attitude will affect the way you see the teaching field as a whole. Remember, it is your favorite subject or you wouldn't be there. If you are interested, you will be interesting. Show your enthusiasm. You may "know" everyone in the class, but do not single out just one even though it may be a close friend to tease or embarrass.

Just because YOUR family is YOUR favorite subject, it does not mean it will be the favorite subject of your class. Their favorite subject will be THEIR genealogy. You, as teacher, may need to be the REFEREE who signals when to change speakers. Using your own family in examples is quite permissible. Examples are the easiest way of showing exactly how a principle works.

LOGISTICS:
Make sure your classroom is comfortable, not too warm or too cold. See that each student understands all the rules, both yours as teacher and the institution rules as well. Are there parking rules? Do your students need parking stickers? These things are usually explained at registration but the first day of class is a good time to review these rules.

EXAMPLES:
Each time a new skill in introduced, an EXAMPLE should be given; if not from your own materials, at least from something you have read or heard about. Explain in depth.

For a time in my teaching career, I began to think I was being too personal. I took out all my own materials and inserted other examples. I found I was uneasy with this method and went back to my own family stories. After all, part of why I had gained knowledge in the field was that my own work had been unusual and interesting. My own work had all the pitfalls and problems that were unraveled by using basic skills expanded.

VOCABULARY:
Use your OWN words! Do not try to use words and phrases that you "think" are more academic. Your own language is fine. Students do not expect you to be a Ph. D. They expect you to know something about genealogy. Speak in the language in which you feel the most comfortable. Do not concern yourself with rhetoric and syntax. If you see a "blank" stare from

your students, back up and rephrase the statement or example in another way. If you are still not getting your point across, ask someone in the room for help. Usually someone is more than happy to help if this situation arises. Fortunately for us, there are fellow genealogists in our audience, and we all know they are ALWAYS the nicest of people. The terminology is not all that difficult. After we have mastered explaining Grantee and Grantor, the rest will seem relatively easy.

TACT:

At the first opportunity, if ever I find a class which teaches TACT, I'll be the first enrollee! Tact in genealogical situations is a most difficult skill to acquire. When confronted with some of the following situations, TACT is needed to answer and direct.

We have all heard this story. "Three brothers came to America. One went south, one went north, and the other went west." Or... "We came from...;"or, "Family tradition states that we descend from General Robert E. Lee's family..."

These and similar stories will stretch your tact. We can gently suggest that the student spend some time in proving these statements. It takes TACT to tell students they must begin from the BEGINNING and prove each fact step-by-step.

Tact may be stretched to the limit when working with that gentleman (and it is usually a man) who wants to research his SURNAME only. Use tact to direct him in the mother's lines as well as the collateral lines. This will be a challenge for you.

PACE:

Pace is the aspect of your speaking voice as it relates to the length of time spent on each lesson within your outline. Your speaking pace will be the area of your personal evaluation that you are able to control. In my case, I need to slow down. Studying your own pace from a recording will give you an idea of where to begin what you might want to change. Reviewing a tape of your presentation may help save time. It may help with preparing an outline. Seldom do we find we are ahead of our outline, we are usually behind. This is because we are trying to fit in new and different examples not mentioned in the outline. Pace is something that comes with experience and using an outline system. So hang in and keep trying.

NOTE-TAKING:

It is an ego booster for the teacher when the entire class begins to take notes. As this happens, and it will, slow down--repeat. It may help if you give advance notice. "This material may be something you want for your files." You may want to write it on the board. This is most important in giving addresses. Look to the student for your guidance. They are your best feedback to what is really getting through to them.

PUBLIC RELATIONS:

That portion of teaching that is mostly unconscious, yet there, that keeps your students coming back for more; that part of teaching that is natural and unassumed -- keeping your students happy is, basically, public relations.

Be prepared to help absentees. We all have our "off" days and when we miss class, we would like to have the material. We can provide that material ourselves, which takes a little extra effort, or we can ask other students to fill them in on what they have missed. This is one trick used in our job of public relations.

Another public relations trick, if your class is two or more hours in length, is to take a break. This is not the time for the students to swarm around your desk and ask questions. Have them stand up and stretch or even take a walk down the hall and get a drink. You will be amazed how this little "break" will help in your teaching.

Treat your students as you would want to be treated. A group taking a prolonged course can and do develop friendships that last a lifetime. Acknowledge this fact and enjoy your new friendships.

TAPING:

Audio and video camera photographing of your class is a decision that is yours. I had always permitted audio taping of my courses. In one class a student taped all sessions and transcribed those tapes. Copies were made for the entire class, typed verbatim. I was shocked. The pauses, language and awkward phrases were all in print. I still permit taping, but ask that it NOT be transcribed. A personal decision!

FOLLOW-UP:

We all give free advice. I have never met a genealogist who didn't give plenty of it. We as teachers give advice all the time. Our knowledge given is a form of advice. Our classes are short-termed, then the students are off to test their wings, like birds leaving a nest. You may find these students will tend to haunt you. Their problems are real. You gave advice and it remains in your memory. Keep a notebook. I label mine "Teacher's Ideas," and describe those problems of interest and their answers. This notebook is a base for other classes. The student with which you have formed this bond should be contacted. He will appreciate the effort. That is not to say you should contact every student in every class, but when an answer or question arises in your mind, call them. It is good public relations.

HANDOUTS AND HOMEWORK

Handouts? How many? What? Ask yourself these few simple questions about handouts..

1. Is this material easily found?

2. Is the material scattered. Did I acquire it from many sources?

3. Would the material be of "keeper" value for the student (material that could be used again)?

Avoid distributing handouts, then reading directly from the material to your classes. THEY CAN READ! Exceptions exist, of course, when the material is detailed and needs further explanation.

Review your budget carefully. If there has been an allotment specifically designed for handouts, use it. Have you asked about a budget for printing? It would surprise you but in many continuing education departments, there is an allotment for just this purpose. They usually require you to go through their printing facilities. They also request specified periods of time for reproducing the materials. Thus, again, we have to PLAN AHEAD. If the society is sponsoring or co-sponsoring your class, ask the questions, up front.

If there is no budget for handouts, PLEASE, NO HANDOUTS. This sounds harsh, but paying out of your own pocket creates a pattern for another teacher. If you put "out-of-pocket" expenses into teaching, the next teacher may refuse because they could not afford the handouts.

Choose your handout materials carefully. It should be designed for INFORMATIVE MATERIALS not easily accessible to the student. The SOURCE should be plainly noted. Not necessarily for the copyright laws, which should be considered, but for your students. They need to know where to get further information on that subject.

All handout materials from your teaching should have your name on it. Original work by you should have your name on it.

Handout material becomes part of the students' file. When working with beginners, you might want to give some suggestions on filing handout material.

The appearance of handouts creates the basis for the type of files created for and by the student. The neater they are, the neater the files will appear. Placement of material on the paper may help to get your ideas across.

When I first began teaching, I tried to get too much material on one page. Placement did not bother me as I was trying hard to get as much material on that page for as little money as possible. As I progressed, I found that the mishmash of materials was confusing the student to the point of distraction. I also found that well- placed material on a page not only looked better (and more professional), but was more easily assimilated by the student. You may want to look through your files and see what accumulated through the years, and make your own judgments.

Handouts designed from materials taken from various printed sources, of the same subject, may need to be retyped or taken to a local print shop and reduced in size and replaced on one sheet of paper. Be careful about reduction. It is a true space saver, but may be difficult to read.

HOMEWORK

Teachers of ADULTS in any situation find better response if students are given the OPPORTUNITY to practice what is heard...the act of DOING is LEARNING. Adult Education departments are advocating the thesis that adults appreciate homework.

My first reaction on homework was WHY and then WHAT? Each individual's genealogy is so different. Wouldn't I just be creating "busywork?"

After much thinking on the subject, all kinds of new ideas began to emerge. Some have been initiated and are working extremely well.

IDEAS FOR HOMEWORK FOR THE GENEALOGICAL STUDENT

The beginning/basic class may be given the assignment to bring to class a family group sheet gleaned from a basic home jurisdiction source, newspaper clipping, picture, obituary, interview, etc., charted and properly documented. These could be evaluated in class either by the teacher or the group. The teacher need not "grade" homework, but the homework can be evaluated and used as a teaching tool.

A more advanced class may be assigned a research log with a proposed research project, or a pedigree problem, bringing it to class with all materials that have been researched clearly defined, then have the students evaluate the work with advice and direction for the researcher to follow. This can take a lot of time, so be careful that everyone is treated equally.

Use your ingenuity in designing homework. A full class participation may be a "contrived" family given to the class and have them prepare a "time line." Or have each student prepare a bibliography of his own location of research. Use your ingenuity to design homework. The possibilities are endless.

AUDIOVISUAL TEACHING AIDS

ANCIENT CHINESE PROVERB

I hear----and I forget
I see-----and I remember
I do------and I understand

AUDIOVISUAL...that art of making use of both hearing and sight in the process of learning. Words are often not enough to get our point across. It is estimated that audiovisual aids increase interest as much as forty percent, make most subjects twenty-five percent more understandable, reduce learning time by twenty-five percent and add to the amount of learning that is retained by thirty-five percent. Like precision tools, however, these devices do not realize these advantages unless they are used with skill. The teacher of genealogy should spend some time planning and using these aids that are available from the educational field, as well as in genealogical education.

We should look at the objective or purpose intended for a specific audiovisual aid. What does it do?

Does it start students thinking on a specific line?
Does it focus attention on a specific point?
Does it spotlight high points of a detailed subject?

If all those answers are yes, you need to think of using audiovisual aids. To learn how to obtain the greatest value from audiovisual material you should review some of the forms available to us and some clues on how to use them.

The physical equipment is usually available at most educational facilities. Schools that have an audiovisual department will be glad to help train you in the use of their equipment. Local office supply houses have most of the equipment and will usually lend it to you if approached as a community service project. Your local library may have equipment that can be checked out or used at their facility.

Ideas conveyed by voice may be misinterpreted unless VISUALLY supported by written words, charts and illustrations.

CHALKBOARD

The old-fashioned CHALKBOARD is still used and, in some cases, upgraded. Many are portable and can be carried with you to class. Some can be leaned against a rail or chair, or placed on an easel. Be careful of the awkwardness of an unstationary chalkboard!

Chalkboard skills and techniques have their value and their limitations. The following are a few rules for the use of chalkboards.

1. Lettering should never be less than two inches high, and larger if possible.

2. Large amounts of materials should never go on a chalkboard. They should be duplicated, except for key words written on the board.

3. Except for "spur of the moment" illustrations, chalkboard work should be prepared in advance.

4. Always be conscious of your audience. Turn toward the class when speaking. Write what is necessary then turn and explain to the class.

OPAQUE PROJECTOR

This audiovisual aid is not used as much as in previous years, but is very effective if you have access to the machine. It is designed to enlarge illustrations. You may put an image, enlarged, from any source, on a screen. The machine is called an OPAQUE PROJECTOR and is not always easily available. Investigate the possibilities in your community.

FILM STRIPS

Commercial film strips are not available to us at this time. We have learned to adapt. Some film strips provided by National Parks and Recreation departments may fit a segment for historical background on battlefields.

VIDEO TAPES

This new innovation for the genealogical community should be used sparingly and wisely, although tapes may certainly bring a new viewpoint into the classroom. The ones that are currently available are not commercial. I see this in the future as a great thing, especially for the isolated areas. Currently they are being filmed from speaking engagements. They are orientated toward the small group since they require the use of a television screen, or screens, placed at advantageous points, so that everyone can see and hear. Video tapes do not lend themselves to note taking since the room should be fairly dark for viewing purposes. They lend themselves well for class discussion.

Video tapes are available professionally for rent or sale from commercial entities and are advertised in various journals and publications. Usually they are advertised under the name of a well-known speaker. Heritage Quest is just one of the companies doing this kind of filming and rental service (see BIBLIOGRAPHY).

CHARTING

FLIP CHARTS...the kind your children use, are easy to make, great to use in small groups and they are easy to carry. They are used when wanting to convey an idea or series of ideas with one key word. The process of describing what events take place in the processing of a probate package makes an excellent example for the use of flip charts. A large cardboard with the key word exposed explains each step of the process as the teacher describes in detail. The KEY WORD helps focus the students' attention on that process.

PREPARED CHARTS...purchased from a company for use in the genealogical classroom are few and far between. Some companies are preparing maps and migration patterns large enough for the classroom but otherwise we must use an opaque projector for most items.

CHARTS...Preparation of charts ranges from simple to elaborate. The simplest chart design may be a pedigree chart drawn on a large poster board. An hour at a local office supply store, or childrens' learning center, will excite your mind on all kinds of new products to be used to help design charts that look more professional. Materials range from inexpensive newsprint to slick polished surfaces in all shapes and sizes.

One of the most effective charts I have seen was cut from the side of a large tissue box, spray-painted and a family tree drawn on the side. It worked well to emphasize the family being deeply rooted, with the branches of the tree of collateral and direct lines being portrayed as leaves and twigs. It certainly answered the question of WHY we do genealogy.

TRANSPARENCIES

This audiovisual aid is currently being used by many teachers because it is available nearly everywhere we teach. The criteria for choosing this method is based on that accessibility and EASE OF USE. Most school media centers maintain a basic collection of transparencies. For the most part, we must create our own in the field of genealogy. The transparency focuses the eye on the screen and directs the mind to the subject.

Some teachers use the overhead projector chiefly as a substitute for a chalkboard. They can prepare at home with a FELT TIP pen or other appropriate marker, writing on cellophane or other clear plastic material, very much as they write on the board. To stop with using just a felt tip pen and nothing else, is to miss some of the exciting experiences possible with the overhead projector. We will discuss principles and ideas to expand your thinking.

THE WRITING MODE: A felt- tipped pen or wide marker that is especially designed for transparencies will keep your work clear, concise and readable. Other materials tend to smudge, especially in transport from place to place. Waxed-based audiovisual pencils, called greased pencils, are available at most office supply stores. These are designed to work on acetate. You can purchase these acetate sheets from an office supply store. The size of the screen is 8 1/2" by 11", just like a typing sheet. There is another special type of acetate sheet called TYPE ON film that may be used directly in the typewriter. I could find this only at a local printer. One clue when using the typewriter is to use LARGE or BOLD FACE TYPE in order to be seen from a distance. A rule of thumb about items on the transparency is that they should always be at least 1/2 inch in height to be seen clearly.

THE SHADOW MODE: This is just what the name implies, a shadow; placing an opaque material on the projector to create a shadow. Genealogically this could be used when we have an item on the projector which we would like to reveal a little at a time. Place a darker piece of material over the film and slide it away to reveal different parts at different times.

Since the transparency use is so common, one wonders if the teacher who uses it extensively is shy. This mode of teaching definitely draws the attention of the class to the projection and off the teacher. It is a great way to enhance the classroom performance of teachers. USE IT!

EVALUATION

The process of evaluation is a matter of choice. We are all "guilty" of personal evaluation in one way or the other. We are quick to criticize ourselves and praise others. Criticism SHOULD mean growth. We are all willing and eager for praise. Praise is a form of EVALUATION.

For personal growth we, as human beings and most importantly as teachers, need to know that we are fulfilling our own personal goals. Are we delivering what is expected of us, or beyond expectations? The process of evaluation should mean a chance for us to grow and to improve.

There are several evaluation forms included for your review. They are designed for various purposes. The student may evaluate everything from the building to the materials and everything in between. One is designed to evaluate the instructor.

When using and reviewing these evaluation sheets, do so with an open mind. They are designed to help, NOT to criticize.

When to evaluate? At the end of the last session. Leave a little time for the forms to be filled out thoughtfully. If taken home to mail, they seldom get back. I personally like to have them unsigned. The student feels free to be honest.

What form? Design your own, or take ideas from the questions that follow. The only rule is to keep it simple.

STUDENT'S EVALUATION SCALE FOR TEACHING EFFECTIVENESS

TEACHER **COURSE TITLE** **DATE**__________

Your honest and thoughtful response to these questions will enable us to evaluate this course/learning activity and will help determine the quality of instruction.

COURSE ORGANIZATION

Little attention as to the work of students, erratic course progress.

Imprecise course goals/classwork lags behind assignment.

Clear statement of class goals, attendance policy/what was expected of the student.

COURSE INSTRUCTIONAL MATERIALS

Indefinite, rambling course presentation.

Sometimes class presentations unrelated to course objectives.

Materials presented match course expectations.

COURSE PRESENTATION

Destroys interest, does little to motivate.

Occasionally motivating and interesting.

Course in clear, intelligent, interesting manner.

INSTRUCTOR PREPARATION

Hesitant, timid, subject seems boring to instructor.

Fairly self-confident, moderately interested.

Interested in subject, well-prepared/well-organized.

SENSE OF PROPORTION

Unsympathetic and inconsiderate of student.

Tries to be considerate, sometimes finds it difficult.

Keeps proper balance, allows questions from students.

Would you take/recommend this instructor for another course?

WORKSHOP SERIES TITLES

Please check the number which best expresses your reaction on each of the following items:

1. The quality of the material presented was:
   (inferior) 1 2 3 4 5 (superior)

2. The subject matter presented was:
   (too simple) 1 2 3 4 5 (too complicated)

3. The coverage of the subject was:
   (inadequate) 1 2 3 4 5 (adequate)

4. Considering the content of the workshop, the mode of instruction was:
   (very ineffective) 1 2 3 4 5 (very effective)

5. The time allowed to ask questions or to seek clarification was:
   (too short) 1 2 3 4 5 (too long)

6. Considering the amount of material covered, the time allotted for each session was:
   (too short) 1 2 3 4 5 (too long)

7. I expect to find this workshop:
   (not at all useful) 1 2 3 4 5 (highly useful)

8. The facilities in which the workshops were held were:
   (very poor) 1 2 3 4 5 (excellent)

9. Overall, I consider these workshops:
   (very poor) 1 2 3 4 5 (excellent)

10. Describe the strongest feature of the workshop series.

11. Describe the weakest feature of the workshop series.

12. Workshop leaders - The leader's knowledge of the subject was:
    (poor) 1 2 3 4 5 (excellent)

13. The ability of the leader to get his subject across was:
    (poor) 1 2 3 4 5 (excellent)

14. The leader's ability to teach the subject was:
    (poor) 1 2 3 4 5 (excellent)

15. The leader's greatest strength was:

16. The leader's greatest weakness was:

TEACHER'S EVALUATION SHEET

Teacher's Name:______________________________________

Course Name: ______________________________________

Please answer the following questions as honestly as possible. It will help in designing future courses.

1. Necessary preparations for the class were made. yes____ no____
2. Classes started on time. yes____ no____
3. Good class discussion, good participation. yes____ no____
4. Discussion kept to topic. yes____ no____
5. Teacher was knowledgeable on the subject. yes____ no____
6. Control of class maintained at all times. yes____ no____
7. Frequent summaries made to crystalize thinking yes____no____
8. Time was permitted for questions. yes____ no____
9. Ability to make students understand was good. yes____ no____
10. Teacher answered questions effectively. yes____ no____
11. Control of class was maintained at all times. yes____ no____
12. Effective use of audiovisual equipment was made. yes____ no____

How Could We Improve This Course?

Would you take another class from this or another instructor in the field, but on a different subject?

OPINION SURVEY

Please give us your honest opinion so that we can upgrade our presentation:

1. Is this your first Seminar? Yes ☐ No ☐

2. I heard about the Seminar . . . ______________________________
____

3. Was parking a problem? Yes ☐ No ☐

4. Did the registration go quickly? Yes ☐ No ☐
   Any suggestions to help us improve?
____
____
____

5. The class periods were: ______________________________
____

6. My favorite instructor was: ______________________________
____

7. What classes would you like to see in the future?
____
____
____
____

8. Would you prefer one major speaker, or several? ______________
   Do you have a suggestion for a speaker? ______________________
____

9. What areas of research are you interested in pursuing?
____
____
____
____

BIBLIOGRAPHY

When it comes to details, we cannot possibly remember everything but we CAN learn where to find those materials needed. A BIBLIOGRAPHY is not designed to be just a list of books and materials available, it is designed to actually give you help. It gives you a place to go for the materials you need. This list is small, but mighty. Each one, in its own way, will help you to be a better teacher.

AMERICAN ASSOCIATION FOR STATE AND LOCAL HISTORY
GENEALOGICAL RESEARCH: A BASIC GUIDE
A technical leaflet #14-1969

Bringham, Charles S.
HISTORY AND BIBLIOGRAPHY OF AMERICAN NEWSPAPERS
1690-1820 2 vols. Worcester, MA
American Antiquarian Society 1947

Beard, Timothy Field with *Denise Demong*
HOW TO FIND YOUR ROOTS
McGraw Hill Book Company

Buckway, Eileen G. comp
UNITED STATES MAP REGISTER
Salt Lake City 1985

Cerny, Johni and *Wendy Elliot*
THE LIBRARY: A GUIDE TO THE LDS FAMILY HISTORY LIBRARY
Ancestry Publishing Company, Salt Lake

Child, Sargent B. and *Dorothy P. Holmes*
A CHECKLIST OF HISTORICAL RECORDS SURVEY PUBLICATIONS.
A BIBLIOGRAPHY OF RESEARCH PROJECT REPORTS:
Gen Pub Co; Baltimore 1969

Colket, Meridith B. Jr.
GUIDE TO GENEALOGICAL RECORDS IN THE NATIONAL ARCHIVES
National Archives 1964

Glenn, Thomas Allen
SOME AMERICAN GENEALOGIES WHICH HAVE BEEN PRINTED IN BOOK FORM IN 1896. Gen Pub Co; Baltimore

Greenwood, Val D.
THE RESEARCHER'S GUIDE TO AMERICAN GENEALOGY
Gen Pub Co; Baltimore

Gregory, Winifred
AMERICAN NEWSPAPERS 1821-1936
A UNION LIST OF FILES AVAILABLE IN THE U.S. AND CANADA
N. Y. H. W. Wilson Co 1937

Eakle, Arlene and *Johni Cerny*
THE SOURCE: A GUIDEBOOK OF AMERICAN GENEALOGY
1984 Ancestry Publishing Co., Salt Lake

Hart, Lois Borland and *J. Gordon Schleicher*
A CONFERENCE AND WORKSHOP PLANNERS MANUAL
Amacom, a division of American Management Association

Historical Records Survey Projects of the W.P.A.
GUIDE TO MANUSCRIPT COLLECTIONS AND INVENTORIES
National Archives

Jacquet, Constant H. ed
YEARBOOK OF AMERICAN AND CANADIAN CHURCHES
Nashville; Abingdon Press/annual

Jacobus, Donald Lines
GENEALOGY AS A PASTIME AND PROFESSION
Gen Pub Co; Baltimore

Kaminkow, Marion J. ed
GENEALOGIES IN THE LIBRARY OF CONGRESS: A BIOGRAPHY
2 Vols; Baltimore; Magna Carta Book Co 1972

Kirkham, E. Kay
A GENEALOGICAL AND HISTORICAL ATLAS OF THE U.S.A.
Salt Lake 1976

A SURVEY OF AMERICAN CHURCH RECORDS
3 Vols; Deseret Books, Salt Lake City, UT

Munsell, Joel's Sons
INDEX TO: AMERICAN GENEALOGIES AND SUPPLEMENT

Rubincam, Milton, ed.
GENEALOGICAL RESEARCH: METHODS AND SOURCES
Washington DC/American Society of Genealogists 1960

Stemmons, John E. and *E. Diane*
THE CEMETERY RECORD COMPENDIUM
Everton Pub., Logan, UT 1979

Wright, Norman E.
KEY TO GENEALOGICAL RESEARCH ESSENTIALS
Provo, Utah; Brigham Young Press 1966 repr Book Craft 1967

KEY TO GENEALOGICAL RESEARCH ESSENTIALS
Provo, Utah
Brigham Young Press, Provo, Utah

The following are materials used to develop CASE HISTORY programs to use in classes to develop case histories and role-playing methods of teaching.

Barclay, Mrs. John E.
"Five Jonathan Dunhams Untangled," T.A.G. 44;4 Oct 1968

Mills, Elizabeth Shown and *Gary B. Mills*
"The Genealogist's Assessment of Alex Haley's ROOTS,"
NGSQ-72:1, March 1984

Moriarty, G. Andrews
"Genealogical Problems," NGSQ, 50:3
Sept 1962 (6 New England & 2 medieval case histories)

Pitman, H. Minot
"Genealogical Proof, Example: Hannah (Knapp) Weed"
T.A.G. 37:4. Oct 1961

Rubincam, Milton
Evidence: An Exemplary Study. A Craig Family Case History
Washington D.C. - National Genealogical Society
Special Publication No. 49, 1981